T0196081

Unfolded

Moments of inspiration
through life's challenges.

ANNETTE D. BURKE

WESTBOW
PRESS®
A DIVISION OF THOMAS NELSON
& ZONDERVAN

WestBow Press books may be ordered through booksellers or by contacting:

WestBow Press
A Division of Thomas Nelson & Zondervan
1663 Liberty Drive
Bloomington, IN 47403
www.westbowpress.com
1 (866) 928-1240

ISBN: 978-1-9736-8994-2 (sc)

Print information available on the last page.

WestBow Press rev. date: 06/22/2020

Contents

Acknowledgment

Easton, Ayden, and Bella you are my heart. I love you more than you will ever know. Each of you is special in your own way, marvelous creations. I admire you as human beings for what you bring to this world. Giving birth to you three are the most treasured moments of my life. Most importantly, I want you to know continually becoming a better mother for you, is my greatest dream. I am so grateful for your unconditional love. Easton, I'm proud of the young man you are becoming.

To my best lady friends, my sisters, you let me be myself authentic and true. You all have been there through so many ups and downs, while we continue to sharpen each other spiritually. I love you for it. Kristy, your faith when it comes to finances and examples of financial generosity has taught me so much. You invited me back to church eight years ago, I said yes. Look what the Lord has done with that one act of obedience. Cindy, you helped me find a backbone and develop my teaching skills for children. Juli, you make me laugh so much! Lisa, Taylor, Sheena, Carol, Dr. Candi, Melanie, Chan man's mom all of you are assets to my life.

Sisters, I only wish I could have found you all sooner.

Thank you, Pastor Jon Walton, for offering leadership and counsel through life's trials and continually reminding me what Jesus would do and how he too experienced great pain. I am thankful for you, Missy, and the kids.

Thank you to Pastor Josh Gerber for taking the time, when I don't know how you found the time; to edit, check my theology, and encourage me to press onward. Your work ethic is an inspiration to me. Your wife Kelli's encouragement and her attitude amidst life's challenges are great wells of hope. I am grateful to God your family moved here.

Thank you, Gary, my friend, for over fourteen years you've been one of the smartest people I know. You've never criticized my life choices, at least not to my face. Thank you for taking the time to be my unofficial unpaid editor along with Pastor Josh without ever making fun of my childlike faith.

Thank you to my State Farm gals whom I would have never made it through those first years of college without. You ladies kept my kiddos free of charge and I am forever filled with gratitude over it.

Becky, fun, and witty, you opened your home when I needed the ministry of hospitality the most. You took a chance. It changed me, forever. The way I felt in your home is the way I want people to feel in my presence, welcomed and unashamed of themselves. Thank you!

Thanksgiving

What do I know about thanksgiving? I know that it has this a way of reshaping our perspective. Giving thanks reminds us to trust, rejoice, depend, and witness even during times when we don't really understand the situations in our life. There was a brief time in my former marriage where I had to choose whether to be bitter or thankful. Every conversation seemed like a dark hole in my opinion. The harder we fought, the worse things seemed. Both of us had a dim perspective on one another. So I prayed. And I cried. I reached out to pastors and friends. It seemed though that everything I tried continued to make things worse. We were at the point where we could not even speak to each other.

One morning I was sitting in my closet. Yes, the closet. I hide in there sometimes to pray, or cry. It's a great place for both. I was on my knees, silently praying; I knew in my heart God could fix this but why wasn't he? It felt unfair. I sat there for a long while before coming to the conclusion that I can't change anyone but me. I searched my heart for anything I might have learned through this trial.

I was so focused on fixing my ex-husband's flaws and changing our situation that I hadn't realized I had some issues too. If I wanted to be thankful and a forgiving person, I should have been praising God for how he made that man, flaws and all. Spending more time focusing on his unique qualities as a human than stewing on the things that had hurt me.

All I will ever have control over is me. Controlling how

I respond to situations is my responsibility. Choosing to be thankful for even the smallest good things, repeatedly, makes the other stuff gently fade away. Jesus said," Let the little children come to me and do not hinder them, for the kingdom of God belongs to such as these" (Mark 10:14). "Praise our God, all you his servants, you who fear him, both small and great" (Revelation 19:5)! God wants his children to thank him any time of the day. Be joyful always, pray continually. Give thanks in all circumstances, for this is God's will for you in Christ Jesus (1 Thessalonians 5:16-18). "Do not be anxious about anything but in everything by prayer and petition with thanksgiving, present your requests to God" (Philippians 4:6)

I am a visual learner so I needed to write things down in order to put thanksgiving in the forefront of my mind. Everyday for several months, I wrote good things about my ex-husband. Anything he did that day that was even remotely good I wrote it down. Then I praised God in secret for it. There were days when we argued and all I could write were things like "God I am so thankful he brushes his teeth," or "God I am so thankful he made the effort and said 'good morning' to me today." God has this way of doing things we never expect. During my time of thanksgiving, God taught me how to respect him for how God made him. Respect didn't start with how I acted, it started with how I thought. I learned to let go of this idea of who I thought he should be. It was as if my eyes had been blind to all the good things he was doing right in front of me. The joy that relationships bring when we choose to love others for who they are, right where they are in their own journey with God is so special. There is just nothing like it. I pray that God opens your hearts to the gift he has given you with those around you, including the people who hurt you. Doing those things didn't fix the marriage, but they helped to guard my heart from the ugliness.

1. What trial or challenge are you facing in your life right now? How are you responding to this trial or challenge, either rightly or wrongly?

2. Read James 1:2-4 and James 1:12-14. How does God intend to use trials, and how can you rejoice in God's purposes in trials? Write down 3-5 ways in which you can rejoice in the trial you are facing.

3. Practice a "Thankful" list. Each day write down 1-3 things you are thankful to God for, and review that list throughout the day. If you have a person on the list, find a different way each day to express your thankfulness for them.

4. Craft your own personal prayer of praise and thankfulness today. For example:

Dear God,

You are worthy to receive glory, honor and praise. You have created all things. Thank you for sending Jesus to save us. Please help us to be thankful today. Please renew childlike hearts in us. Give us a new perspective on our circumstances. In Jesus name, Amen.

My prayer:

Honesty

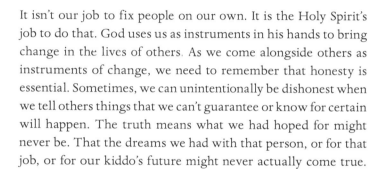

It isn't our job to fix people on our own. It is the Holy Spirit's job to do that. God uses us as instruments in his hands to bring change in the lives of others. As we come alongside others as instruments of change, we need to remember that honesty is essential. Sometimes, we can unintentionally be dishonest when we tell others things that we can't guarantee or know for certain will happen. The truth means what we had hoped for might never be. That the dreams we had with that person, or for that job, or for our kiddo's future might never actually come true. We may never get that house we saw our kids growing up in. There might be an engagement ring we didn't receive. There will always be a life we thought we could have if the other people in our lives would just act differently.

How do we respond when we realize that what we had hoped for may not happen? Maybe it's time to take a firefighter's approach: stop, drop, and roll. Stop thinking about the way things didn't turn out right. Drop to your knees in prayer. Start rolling toward God. You do matter. You are beautiful, and God desires for you to understand his love and care, for you.

Receiving an honest answer is one of the most difficult things we can hear, yet it is also the best. We would love to hear that all our dreams would come true. Even our friends can tell us answers that we like, but aren't necessarily true. None of us know the future, and we can't promise that something will actually happen.

However, God's answer is different. He does not promise

Annette D. Burke

that all our dreams and hopes will come to pass. Rather, his answer is that his kingdom will come, and his kingdom's agenda is far better than anything we could come up with on our own. This is difficult because it means that our kingdom has to die. Our dreams and goals are reshaped and reframed by his plans. God is honest with us as he brings his kingdom plans into our life. He doesn't tell us what we want to hear, but what we need to hear. God's honesty allows us to trust him even when we don't understand what he is doing.

1. Read Matthew 6:9-15. Why is the interruption of Christ's kingdom into our lives actually a good thing? If you prayed for Christ's kingdom to take priority in your life, then what would need to change for that to happen?

2. Ephesians 4:15 reminds us to speak the truth in love. God's answer to us is an honest answer, packaged in truth and love. Consider your conversations this week. In what ways do you struggle either speaking what is true and honest, or doing it in a way that isn't loving?

3. What dreams and hopes do you have that you would like to see come to pass? Craft a prayer asking God, but in a way that expresses thankfulness even where God has different purposes. My prayer:

Truth

When we lie, we often do it to ourselves more than anyone else. Have you ever felt like a victim, or perhaps you felt like life wasn't fair? My most important question for you is, "Who said it was fair?" The reality is, there is only one thing in life that wasn't fair: Jesus giving his perfect and sinless life for our sins. A perfect person's death is not fair.

Could it be that if we could just think about the battles that others are facing more than our own, that our perspective on life and fairness could change? That is a true form of honesty. I had someone lash out at me recently, and it hurt. The first thing I wanted to do was to become angry with that person. The second thing I wanted to do was cry. OK, so maybe I did cry a little. When I got home, I cried through my prayers for that person. I made a choice to believe that this person was going through something that I wasn't aware of. So I prayed for them. When I did, a couple things happened.

First, I felt better. Love thinks the best of others (1 Cor. 13), and I wanted to assume the best. If I allowed myself to be angry for too long I could have lashed out or provided opportunity for the devil (Eph. 4:27). If I did, the circle of pain just keeps going.

The next amazing thing that happened was that my daughter saw me praying. She knew that person was rude to me. She proceeded to sit down beside me as I prayed. I heard her, but I just kept going. She reached out and took my hand. By letting her see and hear my prayers, I can teach her not to be a

Annette D. Burke

victim; not to be the gatekeeper for hate. I can teach her to be an overcomer.

The truth is all about realizing "who" you are, "why" you are here, and "how" to start fulfilling your purpose. Who you are is someone strong enough to stand in the gap for those not quite there yet spiritually. Why you are here is to make a difference in the lives of others. Winston Churchill said "...to change often is to become perfect" so I dare you change often.

I dare you today to become more and more honest with yourself reflecting on times of hurt or anger.

1. Read Romans 12:9-21. Here, Paul makes love the "bookends" for his instructions on our interactions with others. What are 3-5 ways in which you can overcome evil with good this week?

2. Pick 1 characteristic (attribute) of God to meditate on (his love, holiness, goodness, etc)

   - How was this aspect of God encouraging to you in your present situation?
   - What can you do to practice that in your life (starting today, even little things? (this would assume it is an attribute of God that you can reflect in your life)?

Heart Shaping

Five year olds have a funny way of giving biblical perspective. One morning when I was teaching Sunday school we did an exercise with Play-Doh. I handed out the modeling compound to the kiddos and asked half of them to close their eyes, and try to make a heart. I gave verbal instructions to them on how to shape their Play-Doh into a heart. The other half of the kids I didn't give instructions to. Their finished product looked like anything but a heart. Which hearts looked like they were intended to look? The hearts that were guided.

God is good, for he guides us even when we are unaware, and with the concern of how our hearts turn out. The best heart shapers were the ones who could see and be guided. A life being lived without that good guidance from God is a lot like five-year old trying to mold their heart with their eyes closed. It just turns out like anything and everything except what a heart should look like.

What happened with the kids saw the hearts they made with their eyes closed? Hilariously, some of the kids started crying when they opened their eyes because what they saw didn't look like a heart. I got so tickled. But isn't that how we are too? When we realize "Hey, maybe I am doing this wrong," or "Maybe my heart really isn't feeling and causing me to act like it should," that's conviction. But I have great news for you. God isn't like me because he wouldn't laugh at us. Actually, he is that much closer to you when you are humble enough to admit you need him. He is quick to come near when you say "Hey, I can't do this life with my eyes closed anymore".

God deeply cares about our hearts, and getting those right. The good news of the New Covenant that he has brought through the work of Jesus is that we have new hearts, hearts that are able to love and obey him. Consider Ezekiel 36:26. Here, God says, "And I will give you a new heart, and a new spirit I will put within you. And I will remove the heart of stone from your flesh and give you a heart of flesh." Those in Ezekiel's day longed for the time when God would do this kind of heart shaping on them. In our day, we now have these new hearts through Christ.

As you consider your heart and how God is shaping it, answer these questions.

1. What do your desires, expectations, and goals reveal about what is important to you? How might good desires go wrong if we aren't careful?

2. Read Matt. 12:33-35. As you consider the fruit of your life, how does it reveal your heart (whether good or bad)?

3. List some things you say you need, deserve, or are your rights? Write these down, and then compare them to what Scripture says we need, deserve, or are our rights. What differences do you see in what you have and what Scripture says?

Humility

Pride stops us from acknowledging God's grace. It convinces us that we can handle things on our own; that we are stronger in our own power. Proverbs 29:23 reminds us that, "A man's pride will bring him low but a man of lowly spirit gains honor." It's easy to forget about this verse and get a false sense of importance.

One of my dear friends did her job so well, this made her feel a deep sense of pride. She even felt important. A few years ago, she completed certification classes for her job. No one else on her cube floor had the certifications she had. She had even gotten a raise. Over time, she began to think she was more knowledgeable than the rest of her coworkers. Whether it was their efficiency or her skill, this feeling of superiority grew.

Her coworkers saw this attitude of superiority and frankly they were all annoyed by it. When they saw her coming they spread out like flies over an outside dinner. From this women's standpoint, she didn't see a problem. She would correct people when she saw them doing wrong, and she had made herself believe she was helping them. But was she really helping them, or could she have been feeding her pride? Not one person in the office appreciated her help because she lacked humility. Who wants to listen to someone who thinks they are better than you? Not me. I'd say, not you either.

The false sense of importance that pride gives us ultimately brings us low. The temporary things like money, power, prestige and our appearances fade. Those who depend on the Lord gain eternal honor (Proverbs 29:23). What ended up happening to my

Annette D. Burke

friend? She ended up being laid off. While she did make more than the other workers, she was still doing the same job. She found out that she wasn't as necessary to the company as she thought. As hard as it was for her to admit, she knew that it was God's grace and favor which allowed her to do the same job as others and make more money. Those certifications were really just company training. The enemy had deceived her. Her heart had deceived her. Not only that, but her pride deceived her.

Remember that our lives are not our own. They were given to us. Our abilities and wonders we experience are by the grace of God. If you're on the other side of the looking-glass and you're dealing with a prideful person, remember to pray for that person. Have compassion toward them. We all struggle in some way or another. Most of us are just looking for love and acceptance. So the next soul you see struggling, bless them with your anti-pride power of humbleness, and love them even though they are prideful. Have compassion towards them..

1. Think of a recent time you have thought yourself more important than you ought to or when someone else in your life did.

   Write about it below.

2. Ask a friend to identify ways in which they see pride in your life. This might sting, but be willing to accept it. What ways did they identify?

Remember

Sometimes you gotta go back so you can remember how you got where you are now. Or more specifically, "who" got you where you are now, and "who" has been with you all along. It is in remembering we can truly see and be thankful for all that God has done for us.

Anybody remember Jacob? He was the guy that traded his brother a bowl of soup to get his birthright from him. He is also the same guy who fell in love with one woman and married her sister (Leah) because while hustling, he encountered a better hustler who out hustled him. He is also the same guy who had a dream about a stairway to heaven and woke up saying, "surely the Lord is in this place!" He was also the father of Joseph, who wore the coat of many colors. Now, I hope that helps you recall the guy I am talking about today. Can we just go past the Sunday school versions for a minute? Can I just keep it real, and get grown up about the bible for a second?

Jacob had been through some stuff. Who's been through some stuff? Y'all know what I am talking about family issues, relationship problems, years doing work you didn't feel was your purpose? I mean I can't even imagine trying to make two wives happy, let alone wives who were sisters! I surely can't imagine having to clean up the mess after my daughter is raped, and my sons go in and kill everyone to avenge her. Now that is hard-core damage control. Jacob, later known as Israel, is the head of the family, so likely he carried a heavy amount of concern for his family. But God still had plans for him. His story wasn't over. Now hear me, this is huge:

Annette D. Burke

"Even after all he had been through,his story wasn't over. Neither is yours."

Jacob had pulled through. Not only had he survived some stuff, but he came out blessed. Blessed in love, blessed financially, and blessed against his adversaries. He had left a place called Luz and set out for Bethel. This was the second time he had been to Bethel and he was different from the first time.

He was alive and he was blessed. He returned to that place where he had fled to when he was running from Esau, just as God had said. But he wasn't the same. Jacob means "heel grabber" or "deceiver," which is relevant, because the old Jacob was a deceiver. Jacob's story doesn't end with his old name and identity though. In Genesis 35:9 - 10, we read that, "After Jacob returned from Paddan Aram, God appeared to him again and blessed him. God said to him, "Your name is Jacob, but you will no longer be called Jacob; your name will be Israel." So he named him Israel. God had a redemptive purpose for Jacob that he was fulfilling. It didn't come easily for Jacob, but God used all the challenging events and difficulties for Jacob's redemptive good.

Perhaps you have been through some stuff. Or maybe you feel like some days you don't even know who you are. I want to encourage and say Amen! You are not supposed to be that same person. Yes, you are older. Hopefully, you are also wiser, stronger, and more equipped. Growing older in our faith is sometimes like getting older in our natural bodies. There might be some scary times or things that just don't maneuver right. I'd like to encourage you not to waste another minute focusing on who you used to be from the perspective of wanting to be that person again. Rather, remember all that the Lord has brought you through. Remember all those times you shouldn't have made it. Think about those people who just popped up in your life when you needed some encouragement. Do you think that is by chance? No! That was God. That was his divine call on your life. He was whispering to you all the while he was changing you from the old to the new. Your story is unique, and filled with twists and turns. Much like Jacob, you might be a little broken down and older now, but God isn't done with you yet. It is glory to glory my friends.

1. What challenges or hard times have you faced in your life? Write the significant ones down.

2. How have you responded to those hard times? In what areas did you respond well, or what areas poorly?

3. Read Christ's letter to the churches in Revelation chapters 2-3. For each one of the 7 churches, write down what you see in each one of these 3 categories:

    –   The good (what Jesus says they are doing good)
    –   The hard (what difficulties are they facing)
    –   The bad (what do they need to change)

As you look at your life, where do you see these 3 categories? What would Jesus say is good, where would he say you are facing challenges, and in what areas would he say you need to change? Write these down on the rest of the page.

The Battlefield

When I meet with a new volunteer, the first thing I tell them is that if you are not praying in your personal time and are unaware of the spiritual battlefield around you, then this probably isn't the place for you to serve. You're not working on a playground. You are working on a battlefield, with souls at stake. In my opinion, the front lines of battle between good and evil is a place of wounds.

Often, I get a bewildered look in return. Most people have not considered life as a battlefield. Consider what John Piper says about prayer and the battlefield:

"Probably the most familiar passage on the warfare we live in daily is Ephesians 6:12-13.

We are not contending against flesh and blood, but against the principalities, against the powers, against the world rulers of this present darkness, against the spiritual hosts of wickedness in the heavenly places. Therefore take the whole armor of God. In other words, life is war.

But most people do not believe this in their heart. Most people show by their priorities and their casual approach to spiritual things that they believe we are in peacetime, not wartime.

In wartime, the newspapers carry headlines about how the troops are doing. In wartime, families talk about the sons and daughters on the front lines, and write to them, and pray for them with heart-wrenching concern for their safety. In wartime, we are on the alert. We are armed. We are vigilant. In wartime, we spend money differently - there is austerity, not for its own sake, but because there are more strategic ways to spend money than on new tires at home. The war effort touches everybody. We all cut back. The luxury liner becomes the troop carrier.

Very few people think that we are now in a war greater than World War II, and greater than any imaginable nuclear World War III. Or that Satan is a much worse enemy than Communism or militant Islam. Or that the conflict is not restricted to any one global theater, but is in every town and city in the world. Or that the casualties do not merely lose an arm or an eye or an earthly life, but lose everything, even their own soul and enter a hell of everlasting torment (Revelation 14:9-11).

Until people believe this, they will not pray as they ought. They will not even know what prayer is."

Spiritual warfare plays out in all sorts of struggles in life, including additions, poverty, and depression. We don't always think of it this way, however. Remember the story of the possessed man who lived in the tombs mentioned in Mark 5? Night and day this man would cry and cut himself. Once he was free, everyone was astonished because he was dressed normally, and completely in his right mind. While this entire story is fascinating, what sticks out to me the most, isn't the crazy man. It is the sane people. Their fear. We see in Mark 5:14-16 that some witnesses of the whole scene, who saw the naked man that Jesus healed and then a massive pig suicide, went to town and told everyone. The people were not overjoyed that the man was healed. They pleaded with Jesus to leave their region. This is mind blowing to me. What upset these people the most was not the naked man in the tomb who was healed, but the pigs they lost. They missed the point, because they were either overcome with fear or selfishness. At the end of the day, what could be more important than another human life?

I would be doing a disservice if I didn't warn them about what they were signing up for, or that they could potentially be attacked. I have had people walk in claiming to be possessed. I have seen things come against people the minute they decide to serve and fully surrender their life to helping others. This is not an area for the faint at heart.

1. Have you considered life as a battlefield, especially your prayer life? What differences would it make if you did? Write down 3-5 ways in which your prayers or the way you lived would change.

2. Think of a time in which you missed out either rejoicing with someone else or helping them because of fear or selfishness. What did you miss out on, and what did you learn from this?

3. Read Ephesians 6:10-20. Write down 3-5 ways where your spiritual armor is weak. What biblical passages or principles can apply to your weak areas, so that your armor is strengthened?

Warrior

Valiant Warriors have mighty parades because they fight well. They feast at banquets. They care about their health and the safety of their families. There are things you can do to overcome your troubles and challenges easier, but this requires divine help. Here are 4 principles to help you in your spiritual fight.

First, your foundation is your relationship with God. Prayer, fasting, and giving are not optional if you want to live in victory and have a fully fulfilled life. The Bible shows similarity in Matthew 6:2-6,16, "when you fast... when you pray... when you give.." and this means do it and see. These spiritual disciplines aren't optional if you want to be free from things like addiction, eating disorders, depression, chronic illness, or negativity. We have a supernatural God with almighty power, and he calls us to action by his power. Philippians 2:12-13 reminds us of God's work and our work. We are called to work out our salvation, but it's his power that is working in us.

Second, we have to know how to pray effectively. To have a spiritual foundation is to daily renew our minds with the Word of God. We have to pray to God in Jesus' name by which we gain authority to access the throne of grace with boldness. Fullness of life comes from the Spirit of God. The emptiness of that spiritual void that causes us to sin and fall back into cycles of emotional pain or destructive behavior. When we practice the spiritual disciplines, we begin breaking cycles and wrong patterns of living.

Third, you cannot manifest your full potential until you allow the Spirit of God to move, and actively search your heart.

If we are not preparing in his presence we become dulled to elements of the gospel. Psalm 139:23 makes the request that God will search our hearts and try us. This can be frightening, but it's worth it as God changes and shapes our hearts.

Fourth, we have to forgive. Now hold on, I know some of you are saying, "I always forgive." But have you invited the Holy Spirit into your prayer and asked him to intercede to illuminate any un-forgiveness you may have in your heart (Mark 11:25-26)? We are called to forgive as God forgave us (Col. 3:13). As we meditate on God's forgiveness of us, it allows us to forgive others in the way we've been forgiven.

1. Write down all the people's names that come to mind as you pray. Then ask God for forgiveness and pray for him to meet their needs.

2. Set aside a timeframe this month to devote to prayer and Scripture reading. Read either Psalm 119 or the book of Proverbs during this time. Write down aspects that stood out to you from what you read. As you read, pray through each passage as well.

3. What spiritual discipline would you like to grow stronger in developing? Who could help you in this area?

Digging Deeper

Today, I want to tell you about your foundation. The phrase "to teach," in some cases means to pound in, so today I want to "pound in" to you about your foundation so your faith is not like the house was built on sand. Anything built outside the word of God is like sinking sand. Do not be deceived into thinking that it is ok to believe in the friendly verses like John 3:16, and yet ignore the ones that say do not even call someone a fool or even give at the altar if you have a grievance with your brother (Matthew 5:22-24).

How do you go deeper and stronger into your foundation? As I've said, your foundation first must be built on Christ (Matt. 7:24). As this foundation is built on, it must be built with God's wisdom rather than human wisdom. In 1 Cor. 3, Paul contrasts worldly wisdom with godly wisdom. Listen for a minute to what he says. "According to the grace of God given to me, like a skilled master builder I laid a foundation, and someone else is building upon it. Let each one take care how he builds upon it. 11 For no one can lay a foundation other than that which is laid, which is Jesus Christ. 12 Now if anyone builds on the foundation with gold, silver, precious stones, wood, hay, straw— 13 each one's work will become manifest, for the Day will disclose it, because it will be revealed by fire, and the fire will test what sort of work each one has done. 14 If the work that anyone has built on the foundation survives, he will receive a reward. 15 If anyone's work is burned up, he will suffer loss, though he himself will be saved, but only as through fire."

Today know that you will get free from whatever it is you're going through. You are not alone. God didn't create you or put you here on this earth just to suffer. He gave us an instruction manual on how to overcome this world and if we can apply it to our lives we can have victory not just eternally in heaven but here on earth most of the time as well.

1. How would you describe the foundation you are building on? In what ways is it the wisdom of Christ, and in what ways would it be the wisdom of the world?

2. In what areas of your life would you like to grow deeper? List 2-3 of your top priorities.

3. Craft a prayer asking for God to help you go deeper. Such as:

    Dear God,

    Please bless those reading this for their obedience to you and to your word. I pray that they would begin to have secret sins illuminated. Not to beat up on themselves internally or to judge others. That they would see with spiritual eyes how to pray and how to walk abundantly in this world according to your will and your purpose. May we forgive quickly and heal thoroughly by your loving hand. Pound in us the teaching of your word. Give us a fullness of spirit so that we may experience the fullness of life.

    In Jesus name I pray.
    Amen.

Fasting

Your calling and purpose fit it with God's will. We often get scared and think that we can completely mess up God's will for our lives. You can't mess his will up though. God's will, will get done, regardless of our choices. We are not so important that we can thwart God's divine plan. However, the choices we make can determine how fulfilled we live here on this earth. 2 Timothy 1:9 says " He saved us and called us to a Holy Life- not because of anything we have done but because of his own purpose and grace. This grace was given to us in Christ Jesus before the beginning of time." Proverbs 19:21 says that, "Many are the plans in a man's heart, but it is the Lord's purpose that prevails." In Isaiah 55:8 we read, "For my thoughts are not your thoughts, neither are your ways my ways," declares the Lord.

When I meditate on these things, it makes sense to me that I don't understand some things the Bible tells us to do. I don't need to fully understand in order to be obedient. Fasting is one of those things. We need food. It is the opposite of our nature to purposely choose not to eat. Even more to choose the food to eat we like the least. You may have heard there are health benefits from intermittent fasting. What have you heard about the spiritual benefits? While there could be health benefits, the reason we fast is to remind us we need the bread of Jesus more than physical bread.

In a spiritual storm, there are things you can do to get control of your feelings. What we need to do is to shift our season. I do believe depending on how desperate you are for a miracle, or to see things change in your life or the lives of those you love, you will prove your obedience regardless of the season. Maybe you have a child who is addicted to prescription medications, maybe you are desperate for resolve in your marriage, or wisdom in your finances. If you want it bad enough you will sacrifice. The sacrifice is about trusting God to meet your needs.

Remember, fasting isn't a manipulation tool to get God to do what you want. Rather, it is a way to gain spiritual clarity, and to take back a foothold to the things we cannot see that control us. It is a way to overcome our emotions and starve our flesh to regain and retrain our self discipline muscles.

Years ago, I was working in fast food as a manager. I hated it. I loved the people I worked with but I just hated seeing my children or having to depend on food stamps. I wanted a better life. I prayed and prayed for it. But I didn't see much change. I was consistent in prayer, praying countless times a day for at least two years, but still seeing no way out. I applied for jobs and got no phone calls. I was working 50+ hours a week, trying to go to school at night, and felt like I hardly saw my babies at all. This was a crucial time because they were so small. As a single mom, many nights I cried, "Lord, how will we make it? How can I give them a better life?" Then my pastor did a series on spiritual warfare. It lasted several weeks, but the week he talked about fasting a light bulb went off inside my head. That was the only thing I hadn't tried. I love food, but I hated working fast food more. Friends if you get desperate enough you will either give up or give in to God.

I read about Daniel. When the angel came to him he told him that his prayer was heard the minute he spoke it. But the spiritual war—the battle we can't see, had delayed his answer (Daniel 10:10-20). I have had so much trouble in my life that I knew after reading the story, there were things which I may never understand working against me. I also knew some of it was me. So I kept praying and this time I fasted. I did the Daniel fast. I got a couple of my sisters from the church to do it with me. Just a few months afterward, I got a random phone call from someone I hadn't spoken to in more than five years, offering me a job because their mom was hiring. What are the chances? I went from a crazy schedule to normal business hours. I went from food stamps and government housing to buying my own groceries and renting a better home. I was thankful those things were there to help me when I needed them, but I was so much more thankful to be free! Not only did I get a job I hadn't even applied for but I wasn't even qualified. The owner paid for my licenses and equipped me with the certifications I needed to do the job.

God does even more than you ask. He will bless you even more than you dream. He, like any good father, wants to bless you. You will still have troubles, but you will be blessed along the way. If God brings new blessings into your life he will equip you to handle it.

I am not any more special or favored than you. I know God has amazing things in store for you just like he did for me. I believe it. So I just want to ask you today, what will you give up to get clarity, to get your divine answer? Do you believe that you will be blessed? Do you truly believe you will be free? No matter what I say, or anyone else says, you have to believe first.

God does answer prayer. I have seen it many times. We are not defenseless. Be diligent. Be valiant. Be the you that you were created to be. It is time to get serious about God's word. It is time to believe the whole Bible, not just the warm and fuzzy parts. You're not alone, and you can do this no matter what you are going through and no matter how you feel.

1. Have you tried fasting for a spiritual reason before? Describe what it was like, and how you benefited from it if you did try it. If you haven't tried it, what are some of your reservations?

2.   Make a plan to fast once this month. It doesn't have to be a long fast (even 1 meal). Have a spiritual plan during this time of fasting (what you will read, pray, etc) so that your focus is on the Lord.

3.   Look up some biblical passages describing and discussing fasting. What do you learn from those passages?

Keep Going

You are not alone if you are struggling right now. Perhaps you have lost a loved one or maybe you're lonely in your relationship. I want to tell you that God has a plan for you. Today, I pray you will find your courage to keep going. When we find disappointment after disappointment we start to hear that faint whisper of "give up" in our ear. But that is not God's plan for you. He didn't bring you to this season of life for you to quit. He is bringing you through this so that you may help others. It's cliche, but it is so true that iron is forged in the fire.

How was your last Thanksgiving holiday? I don't know about you, but the holidays are hard when you are in a season of depression or trauma. Maybe Thanksgiving wasn't what you thought it would be. Maybe you felt alone even when you were with lots of people. Some of us may even have felt disappointment set in the day after Thanksgiving because of how much we ate, or because of what is left in our bank account! Regardless of what causes your disappointment, have courage.

I want to share a story of a young lady who endured years of suffering on the inside. She had an eating disorder. It seemed that the holidays were the hardest time for her, but not because of all of the food. The reason was because she felt even more unnoticed and even more alone. There she was wasting away on the outside, and hurting from emotional pain on the inside, and she felt like no one saw.. She had lost about thirty pounds since the last time her family saw her, and no one said a word. The family home where turkey dinner was served was buzzing with noise and delicious smells. Laughter could be heard from the street, and children were running around at what seemed to be a joyful family gathering. But here was my friend, off in a corner couch looking down at her phone, contemplating her death. How did this sad girl go unnoticed?

I do know that she sat in the corner and wondered if anyone would even miss her if she ended her life. Unlike everyone else who was merry and talking about all that was going on in their own lives, this teen was planning her escape. She didn't take her own life, but she did an experiment with self harm. Praise God she opened up and was able to find healing. From this I'd like you to learn two things.

First, keep noticing. Pay attention to everyone around you. Many people find the holidays to be hard. Let us not be so consumed with our own plate of food or our own lives so much so that we don't notice everyone in the room. There is someone out there today, a sister in Christ who needs to feel loved, accepted, forgiven and you are just who God is sending to bless them with it.

Second, keep going. If you are like this girl we talked about, please don't look around this holiday and feel sad. But rather look up. Look toward the heavens to a father who loves you and very much wants to be with you while you're hurting. You can't get healing from what you don't open up about. Tell someone what is happening inside you. If you can't open up to anyone in your circle, then seek professional help.

1. Read Hebrews 13:5-6. What encouragement does this passage bring you? What difference could believing it make in your life?

2. Write this scripture on a note card or tape it to the back of your phone. If you feel those thoughts or emotions

that hurt, pull it out and remind yourself that God is with you, and he isn't going anywhere regardless of how you feel.

3. List one thing you are thankful for that has always been in your life. It could be a person, a bad habit you learned from, it could be a quirky unique thing about you, even a blanket, or it could be a loved one. Use these last few minutes of time to think about and meditate in that feeling of gratitude. Or write about a holiday experience good or bad. Who was in the room? Did you pay attention to everyone?

4. Write out Hebrews 6:19. What encouragement or help does this passage bring you?

Soul Anchor

No matter how many storms I go through in my life, I am reminded each time that Jesus is the steady anchor, even when my ship's sails are torn. The first time I needed an anchor in life was when I learned that my mother was murdered by my father. I was six, and was scared, but Jesus was there. Through years of abusive relationships and a teenage pregnancy, I tried to substitute other anchors like alcohol, but looking back I know Jesus was there loving me. The surrogate saviors that I used to steady and calm myself failed me in the storms of life. I trusted the wrong things, and as a result my ship crashed repeatedly. This led me to carry two things around even after I recovered from the wrecks of the past, namely bitterness and fear. I had the fear of people because they had hurt me. I had bitterness towards those that I had seen do evil with no regret, and where I didn't see justice enacted. As a result, my guilt and shame weighed down on me.

When I hit rock bottom I finally realized that Jesus was there. I discovered he had been there all along, since I was six years old. From the moment I had walked down that altar, he had been protecting me even from those who meant to harm me. He was also protecting me from myself and the consequences of foolish choices. His grace and mercy were abounding in so many areas in my life. When my adoptive parents didn't want me anymore, God put other people in my path to mentor me. I found him to be a true and faithful father to the fatherless, who never let me down like others did.

His steady hand continued to guide and protect me throughout life. When I was in high school, I hit a light pole going fifty-five miles per hour in a thirty zone. It was during a fight with a boyfriend (from one of those relationships I shouldn't have been in). Only by God's grace did I walk away unharmed. His goodness and protection continued during years of reckless living and parties where I could have died from endangering myself. Often, I probably should have died from being foolish, but God was there. No matter what or how I messed up, God's grace and mercy were always sufficient for me. He gave me a way out of my sin and the grace to navigate the consequences. When I thought I could never finish college, God put my face on a billboard, for the college! Finally, I had found my true anchor in Jesus Christ. He is where I draw my hope. There was a difference from storms early on and storms after I knew God.

Today I am praying the same for you. Whether you have just been diagnosed with an illness, are suffering in your marriage, worried about your child's addiction, or suffering in your finances, you can find an anchor in Jesus. Everything else in this life will let you down. People will let you down. Your money will disappoint you. Your friends and family may at times hurt you, but I can assure you that God cannot tell a lie. God loves you. He treasures you. He provides for you. He watches over you. He asks in return that you have faith. It is hard when we don't know why, but sometimes the why is so we are forced to trust in nothing less than Jesus. You will overcome this storm if you have an eternal anchor. An anchor is the very thing that keeps you steady and grounded even in risky waters.

At a women's conference I gathered we all have an anchor, only our anchor is either tied to what is below or it's tied to heavenly places with divine power and access to the lighthouse of grace. Someone needs to hear this today. You will make it through this storm. Your circumstance does not define you. Start bringing peace to your situation today by finding your anchor in Jesus.

1. Write out Jeremiah 17:5-8. Draw a picture of a shrub in a desert, and a flourishing tree. Under each picture list:

   – What kind of plant is this?
   – Why is the plant like this?
   – In what ways am I like this plant?
   – In what ways would God have me change?

2. Read Proverbs 29:25. Write down 3-5 ways in which you tend to put your trust in other people or things instead of God, to get their approval or to please them. What happens when you do this?

3. How have you experienced other people hurting or failing you? Write down some ways in which you have responded to this hurt. How would God have you respond, and what steps do you need to take if you have not responded in a biblical way?

Mind set

Have you ever been dead tired? I mean, so dead tired that you wouldn't hear a freight train if it rolled over your head, or a marching band playing straight in your ear. I had this experience one morning. I woke up feeling ready for anything, even taking on the world. But by lunchtime, all the negativity had taken its toll. If my energy was dynamite, I didn't feel like I had enough to blow my nose. It seemed that anything that could go wrong, did go wrong. Have you ever had a day like that?

When I started my day, I expected a blessing. I was joyful and had even started humming on my way to work. What changed? My mind-set had changed from joyful to sadness. It started when I learned of the death of someone that I knew my entire life. I forgot about the hope of what kind of day I would have, because all I could think of was the sadness that this family would now be facing. Then, it seemed everyone I came in contact with was like the grinch. I let the negativity of others drain me. I didn't keep my mind at peace, and I joined in on being negative.

When I arrived home, I realized I still had to make dinner. I began thinking, "I can't-I just can't today." Suddenly, there was a knock at the door. Irritated, I thought, "what did our dog do now?" I was ready to break down when I opened up the door if I heard one more piece of bad news. But when I opened the door, it was a friend from church standing there with a pizza. Now, I hadn't talked to this person that day. She didn't know what kind of day I was having, but there she stood with a big bright smile. I tell you, that pizza smelled better than any perfume I had ever

Annette D. Burke

tried! I asked her, "what are you doing here?" I tried to think if I had talked to anyone about my bad day, but didn't remember doing so. She said, "The Lord just told me to bring it so I did!" and she turned around and left, faster than my kids do when I bring out the chore list.

Then it hit me. The strength I needed to finish homework with my kids and fold those clothes returned. It was like the breath of life was breathed right back into me by that one act of kindness. I truly felt God's love. As I shut the door and turned the dead bolt, I had tears streaming down my face, but it was of joy because I was reminded once again how dependent I am on God. Also, I was reminded of how faithful he is to me. Just like it says in Zechariah 4:6: "So he said to me, "This is the word of the LORD to Zerubbabel: 'Not by might nor by power, but by my Spirit,' says the LORD Almighty."

That word spirit is referring to "breath." It was not by my own might nor my own power, or by even my friend's might or power that I made it through that bad day. It was only by the Spirit of the Lord. If you're struggling, the Spirit of God will move in your life. It can be hard to remember that, especially on those bad days, but be expectant and God will be faithful. You will begin to see things differently. You will begin to notice all the ways God's breath flows right into your circumstances.

1. What are your thoughts and feelings like today? Write down as many of them as come to your mind.

2. Read Phillipians 4:8. Write down the ways in which your thoughts line up with this verse, and the ways in which they don't. For the ways they don't, what truths in God's Word do you see that could change the way you are thinking?

3. Craft a prayer based on Phil. 4:8. Make it a renewed thought that is combined with thanksgiving to replace your old thought. For example:

Lord, I am struggling today. My situation seems as if everyone is against me. Please help me to remember that in your Word, you have said you are for me. You have told me that you are my rock and stronghold in times of trouble. Thank you for being this refuge when all my other idols fail. In Jesus name, Amen.

Wilderness

"Alone in the wilderness...that is what I am," said my friend as I gave her a huge hug. She had been in this season of life for a long time. I can imagine how it felt for her. This wilderness season had come and gone in my own life and was all too familiar. The experience feels like you are going around in circles and not getting anywhere. It's almost as if you are driving but the GPS isn't working, and you have no idea where to go. I'd like to tell you a series of stories about women who experienced a wilderness season. A season where being alone, lied to, and feeling out of place in their own lives seemed never ending. Then, I want to give you hope and point your focus upward to the one who can bring you out of it, and into the land of fruitfulness. The wilderness is where you keep going around and around, never getting to where you are supposed to be. I want you to get to where you are supposed to be. I want you to find contentment.

The first story takes place in ministry. Ministry is often a place where it is hard to work alongside people and groups, who at times seem nothing like us. The particular struggles and challenges they face are ones in which we seem to handle with ease, so we can't imagine how it could even be a struggle for them. For one woman, Susan, ministry became a wilderness experience. Susan found that displaying compassion was extremely hard for her. She knew her ministry or God's ministry, was ultimately not hers, but God's. She had always been honest, maybe even to a fault. Then, she was called to walk alongside someone who struggled with lying. She valued honesty as a virtue of utmost importance in her life, so it was extremely difficult to come alongside someone failing in that area. She had many thoughts, such as, "How could anyone flat out lie? What are you going to do when the next temptation they face is to lie about you? Do you stand your ground? Do you call them out on their lies one on one? Do you involve other people to expose this sin?" As a Christian living in a sinful world, it should be no surprise that any of these dilemmas would happen to Susan.

Sure enough, they did. Sadly, Susan was hurt by the lies of others. They left her ostracized from her own ministry, alienated from her own church family. While all she really wanted was to love, protect, and hold another Christian accountable, things did not go this way. When she was hurt, she now had to face the choice of how to respond. Would she leave the church? Would she give up? Or would the experience drive her out of the wilderness and into the rest of the Lord?

The second story is of a woman who was so good at her job. She took a great deal of pride in what she did, making sure not to make mistakes, and to always be on time. She gave her best to each and every customer. Because of this woman's past experiences, she always feared someone would think she was the reason if the numbers were off at work. She was afraid she would be accused of stealing. One day, the numbers were off. When she was asked by her supervisor about it, she didn't even put up a fight. She didn't wait around for them to fire her. She simply didn't go back to work. She was innocent, but enemy had been rendering her defeated long before her accusation came about. There she was in the wilderness. Job after job. Living her own self fulfilling prophecy.

My third story is about marriage. A lovely lady was incredibly devoted to her husband. While she did have an unpleasant past, that was not who she was anymore. As a gorgeous and super friendly person, she easily attracted others. Her husband noticed this, but she was not aware of it. She meant no harm, for her personality and character made it easy for others to speak with her. One day, someone from her past sent her a message. The message made it seem that they had been communicating, even when they had not. Her husband discovered the message and did not believe her. The woman had nothing to stand on except her word, and the husband refused to believe her. He left angry. Stunned and hurt, the woman sat there alone. She thought, "why shouldn't I cheat if I am being accused anyway?" As she continued to dwell on the tempation, she eventually did. There she was in the wilderness.

In all three of the stories, my friends were right in the beginning. They started off with good intentions, but drifted away in the wilderness season. What do we do differently, especially when we have entered into a season of wilderness and feel lost? We press in. We do the things we haven't been doing. So today I want to tell you that what you are going through is a mere opportunity. Not an opportunity for your heart to grow cold, not an opportunity to throw in the towel, not an opportunity to do less or be less committed. This season of wilderness is an opportunity for you to produce fruit. It is an opportunity for you to make the right decision, and stand in divine power without complaining about being here again.

Wilderness experiences are an opportunity for the friend in my first story to show the fruit of forbearance and love regardless of feeling. For my second friend, to remain faithful and produce goodness along with kindness at that job even when she was questioned. My third friend had the opportunity to be gentle with her husband who thought wrong of her. She could produce self control regardless of her feelings, and stand firm, knowing the truth.

1. Write down where you are at. What wilderness season are you facing now? How are you responding?

2. Read the account of the Israelites in Exodus 16 and
    Numbers 14. What difficulties did they face? How did
    they respond to the wilderness challenges? In what
    ways are your responses similar and different? What
    can you learn from this?

3. Make a list of ways to respond differently in your
    wilderness season. For example:

    •   We pray harder. (1 Corinthians 14:15).
    •   We do the opposite of giving up. (Luke 18:1).
    •   We go against the way of the world. (Romans 12:2).
    •   We give not just what they took, but we give our
        all. (Matthew 5:40, Luke 6:29).
    •   We turn the other cheek. (Matthew 5:39).
    •   We stand strong and know that God himself will
        fight for us (Exodus 14:14).

Believe

Today, I want you to think about your beliefs. What do you believe about yourself? Generally, are your beliefs about yourself positive or negative? I hope when you think of yourself that it is in a positive and honest way. I hope you can find joy and humor in all the little unique things you do, that make you into you. I want you to thank God for them. Especially for the weird things. I know you've got them. We all do.

God wants his children to pray and thank him every time of the day. We read in 1 Thessalonians 5:16-18, "Be joyful always, pray continually; give thanks in all circumstances, for this is God's will for you in Christ Jesus." What you think about and believe will set the direction for your day. Our beliefs about God and how he is working in our lives will affect the way we view ourselves and our purpose. When we think wrongly about God, we will also think wrongly of ourselves. Let's consider a couple of essential truths about God to keep in the forefront of our minds, that will ground and stabilize us.

First, God is good and comforts us. Observing children interact with each other reminds me of these truths. I get so proud of those kids when they are quick to assist one another. That is exactly what happened with our little Play-Doh experience, that I talked about earlier in heart shaping. The kids who had the privilege of having their eyes open went straight to the rescue of the other kids. It wasn't even more than five minutes, and they had everyone's dough molded to match. They were all on the same playing field now. I thought, "These kids are so amazing". We can learn so much from them. They didn't brag about how they had an extra opportunity. They didn't ask why they had to help. They simply saw a need and went to work, no questions asked. The other kids hadn't even asked them for help. They had just merely started whimpering, and immediately they had help. God does that for us.

Second, God is good, and he restores us. In Psalm 107, we see four groups of people. Three of these groups fall into trouble because of their own sinful actions. The fourth group lands in trouble because of life in a fallen world. The solution for each one of these groups of people is to remember the steadfast love of the Lord. As they do, God rescues them from their situations. God is in the business of restoring people.

1. Read Romans 12:3. What does this verse teach us about viewing ourselves? In what ways do you struggle with thinking more highly of yourself than you should?

2. Read 2 Corinthians 12. Paul's concern in verse 6 is that others will think more of him than they should. What surprises you about this concern of Paul? Why do you think we have the opposite problem, in wanting others to think more of us than they should?

3. Pick out a person today and make a list of ways in which they are unique, and aspects about them that you appreciate. Let them know at least 2 of those ways, to encourage them in their day.

4. Write down some ways you are unique, and how God has gifted you. How can you use these traits or areas to serve God and others?

Press ON

I think that the hardest time to serve others is when we are going through emotional damage control. During times like these, we might not see as much fruit as we would like in many areas of our lives. This makes it even harder to just keep going. It makes it hard to even keep a smile on our faces. I know this because I have been there. I remember the moment when I found out my first husband was still married, the moment I knew I had a miscarriage, the moment when my family member died. I was there. Friend, one thing I don't want is for you to stay there in that dead place. Today, I want to share with you how to recover.

The Walking Dead is a tv show in which a zombie apocalypse has occurred, and people are merely trying to survive. There are a couple of main characters, who like me, were going about serving others, but struggling because of the lack of visible fruit. I don't agree with everything about the show, but it is a great visual of how the pruning and fruit bearing process works. Rick, the main character, is in an environment that cultivates fending for oneself. Yet, he consistently is concerned about the group as a whole. People are doing ruthless things all around him, but he keeps the goal of helping others survive in center focus. When his focus drifts off, people die. He struggles because he never sees any fruit for his efforts, but only more trouble.

The Christian walk is similar in the fact that we can go through seasons of life where fruit is hard to see. Seasons can feel like they are only filled with death, tears, and pain. But I promise you that God is still there. He is still working in your life. What if our spiritual life was like the Walking Dead? What if the minute we took our eyes off Jesus and serving others, people started to die? In reality, the very moment in which we are distracted from our relationship with Jesus, that once flame of passion reduces down to a barely lit ember. It is difficult to remember joy in times like these. When our flame goes out because we forget why we are here, it begins affecting everyone else around us. Those we were supposed to encourage remain defeated. We could have had purpose and passion, but end up settling for a life filled with meaningless nothing. I don't want this to be you. If you are hurting today, please don't give up. Don't give up on your ministry. Don't give up on your kids. Don't give up on your family or your spouse. Most of all, don't give up on God. He has not left you. He is still there. He is still good. Stay focused. Your joy won't remain gone forever. Today you can start to get it back. How? By remembering the God of your salvation.

1. Read Habakkuk chapter 1. What are Habakkuk's complaints? How can you relate to his complaints? What is God's response in chapter 1? Why might this response seem strange?

2. Read Habakkuk chapter 2. What does he say in verse 3? In what ways can you apply verse 3 to your situation? What warnings does God give? How does this encourage you to keep pressing on, as you are reminded that God will take justice at his proper time?

3. Read Habakkuk 3. How is he encouraged in his prayer? In verses 17-19, what does he do to find encouragement?

4. Craft a prayer today like Habakkuk does. Write your prayer below.

Hearing God

Let me start off by saying that to hear God's voice is to get direction in your life. It means that the one who created you is giving you guidance in the day to day choices you have to make. If someone says, "God told me," it does not typically mean they hear an actual voice. In biblical times, God spoke to people in ways that are different from today. He used angels, a burning bush, plagues, death, a flood, people or prophets, and even a donkey to get his message across. While God can speak in various ways today, the way he has promised is through his Word. We will never go wrong when we listen to what he says in his Word.

How is it that we get off track from hearing God correctly? The answer is sin. Sin has distorted our knowledge and understanding of who God is. What happens when you don't know someone to the fullest extent, or have a wrong perception of them? What happens when you enter into a relationship and misunderstand the other person's character? The result is that the chances of misinterpreting their actions or what they are trying to say increases. Let's talk about how that relates in real life.

Take a marriage for example. Two people, who are so in love after marriage, try and assist each other. The wife tries to help by offering her husband advice on various things. She means well, and is lovingly trying to help. But she doesn't fully know him. At the same time, sin distorts the perspective of her husband. He interprets her advice as thinking she wants to change him because he is incapable or inadequate of handling things on his own. He does not understand love from her point of view. So he takes this loving woman's message wrongly, and interprets it as disrespect. When he responds sinfully towards her, she feels unloved, and responds sinfully in return. As a result, the cycle of hurt contines.

Often, it is the same with our relationship to God. This means that never reading his Word, or not learning about the culture and time when he spoke to his people, or failing to rightly grasp his character means that we are vulnerable to misunderstanding him. Let's face it, the Bible is huge. Even if we memorize half of it, then when we learn the other half, some of what we already learned we have already forgotten. That is why it is so important to read God's word on a regular basis, because hearing his voice and truly knowing him comes when you read his Word.

If someone tells me, "God told me to not pay my tithe because a had a lot of bills this month," I would say, "Honey, I love you, but I don't think that was God, because he has always said give to him first, then he will take care of your needs." Please don't hear me judging. I am merely encouraging a deeper understanding of who God really is (1 Kings 22:5 ; 2 Chronicles 18:4, 31:6, 31:12, & 31:5, Matthew 6:33, Malachi 3:8-10, Leviticus 27:30-32, Numbers 18:21,24,26,28, Deuteronomy 12:6,11,17, 14:22,23,24,26:1, Nehemiah 10:37-38, 12:44, 13:5,12). If you know him, you will know if he would have said that or not.

I will use myself as an example. People who truly know me would doubt a rumor that last week I punched someone in the face, or that I said it was ok to never read your Bible. Why? Because they know me and they know that goes against my character. They can tell if that is something I would be likely to say because of who I am. It is the same in your relationship with God. Would he tell me to give my last $5 dollars away? Absolutely. How do I know? Because he has mentioned how he treats people who give when they have nothing. He has told us how he is faithful to those who trust him.

A very wise woman I know was having some trouble in her marriage. Her husband had become harsh and distant from God. Everyone was telling her to get a divorce. She said she knew God was telling her to stay in the marriage. I asked her why, and she said, "Because I know God. I know how he feels about divorce. I know what he says about the covenantal nature of marriage, even when I don't feel like loving. I know that God would say to show grace and love, because that's who he is."

I wasn't where I am in my faith today, and I think I might have even rolled my eyes at her response. But years later, after countless more sleepless nights in prayer, and tear filled sobs, over an open Bible, I know. I know that God is good. I know that he gives chances, second chances, third chances. He shows mercy and grace. I know that he is near to the broken heart. I know God blesses those who seek him first. I know that like any good parent, he allows consequences when we repeatedly disobey, and puts faithful people in our path to help us see his love. But most of all I know that he loves us, all of us. When I am unsure or have any doubt if it's his voice or not, I know that I can look to what he has done in the past. I can look to what he has said in his Word regarding that circumstance or situation or sickness. His Word doesn't change. God's character doesn't change. He remains yesterday, today, and tomorrow.

1. Read Genesis 3. What went wrong with Adam and Eve? What happened when they listened to another voice, another interpreter? How can you relate to what happened to them?

2. Read Psalm 119. Write down all the benefits you see from knowing God through his Word.

3. Memorize one of the following verses. Tape it to your phone so you'll be reminded of it throughout the day.

- In the morning, Lord, you hear my voice; in the morning I lay my requests before you and wait expectantly. Psalm 5:3
- I love the Lord, for he heard my voice; he heard my cry for mercy. Psalm 116:1
- Listen and hear my voice; pay attention and hear what I say. Isaiah 28:23
- Here I am! I stand at the door and knock. If anyone hears my voice and opens the door, I will come in and eat with that person, and they with me. Revelation 3:20
- Then I heard another voice from heaven say: "'Come out of her, my people,' so that you will not share in her sins, so that you will not receive any of her plagues; Revelation 18:4
- My people have been lost sheep; their shepherds have led them astray and caused them to roam on the mountains. They wandered over mountains and hills and forgot their own resting place. Jeremiah 50:6

Measuring Goodness

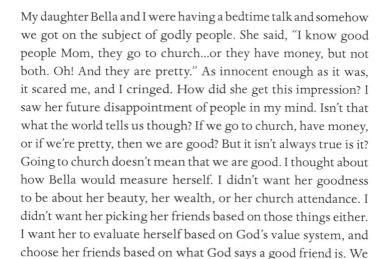

My daughter Bella and I were having a bedtime talk and somehow we got on the subject of godly people. She said, "I know good people Mom, they go to church...or they have money, but not both. Oh! And they are pretty." As innocent enough as it was, it scared me, and I cringed. How did she get this impression? I saw her future disappointment of people in my mind. Isn't that what the world tells us though? If we go to church, have money, or if we're pretty, then we are good? But it isn't always true is it? Going to church doesn't mean that we are good. I thought about how Bella would measure herself. I didn't want her goodness to be about her beauty, her wealth, or her church attendance. I didn't want her picking her friends based on those things either. I want her to evaluate herself based on God's value system, and choose her friends based on what God says a good friend is. We had a long conversation about love that night.

Here's what we need to know about goodness. One time a man went up to Jesus, and called him the good teacher. Jesus reminded him that no one is good except God. Yet, the man still thought he could be good enough to keep the law. Jesus had to show him that this wasn't true, for he could never be good enough. Now, this may sound like bad news to you. If I can never be good enough, then what's the use of trying anything? That's not what Jesus meant though. He means that apart from his work in our lives, we have no goodness on our own. Any goodness we have is only because of him.

I can tell my daughter that she can do good to others because of God's help. In Matthew 7, Jesus speaks of good fruit coming from a good tree (or heart). When our hearts are changed, we are able to do good to others. Goodness is a fruit of the Spirit (Gal:5), and a responsibility we have toward others (Gal. 6:10). I want my daughter to show goodness to all she comes in contact with, and to pick friends who do the same.

1. How do you measure goodness? In what ways does it line up with what Scripture says, and in what ways is it different?

2. How do you measure your life in terms of it being successful or not? What marks a good day or a bad day from you? In what ways would Jesus approve of the value system you use, and in what ways would he correct it?

3. What are 3-5 ways in which you can grow in showing goodness to others? Write these down, and put these into practice this week.

Big Dreams

When I was writing my first book, I was so excited. I felt like God had given me a vision and that I was going to be an awesome writer. I told all my friends, "I am writing a novel. And I feel like God is going to bless it." A few months went by, and I was knocking out the pages like a heavyweight boxer takes out a novice. I had outlines, chapters, and plots coming out of my ears. The more I wrote, the bigger my dream became. It was like a balloon that wouldn't stop expanding! When I got past about one hundred pages, I felt like I had arrived. Nothing could stop me now. Then, it seemed like the book took all my focus. It even took some focus away from God. This was ironic, since I was doing this for God.

I had poured my all into the book, even asking people to proofread it for me and give me their honest opinion. But before I gave them a copy, I built it up like a skyscraper. I went on and on about how thought out the characters were, the story line, and its complexity. I knew (really knew) they would love it. I will be gracious to myself and say...at least they didn't hate it! But the weeks went by, I would ask them, "Have you finished it yet? What did you think? Did you get to this part?" I was utterly perplexed that they were able to put it down. By put it down, I mean they could hardly read it. I had made it sound so marvelous there was no room for critique, only let down. It felt like I had a picture of the future and I wanted everyone to be as excited as I was about it. They just weren't. Well, this had me thinking of a story in the Bible. It happened to Joseph in Genesis 37. Here we read:

Joseph had a dream, and when he told it to his brothers, they hated him all the more. 6 He said to them, "Listen to this dream I had: 7 We were binding sheaves of grain out in the field when suddenly my sheaf rose and stood upright, while your sheaves gathered around mine and bowed down to it."8 His brothers said to him, "Do you intend to reign over us? Will you actually rule us?" And they hated him all the more because of his dream and what he had said.9 Then he had another dream, and he told it to his brothers. "Listen," he said, "I had another dream, and this time the sun and moon and eleven stars were bowing down to me."10 When he told his father as well as his brothers, his father rebuked him and said, "What is this dream you had? Will your mother and I and your brothers actually come and bow down to the ground before you?" 11 His brothers were jealous of him, but his father kept the matter in mind. (Genesis 37:5-11 NIV).

Joseph's dream was decades away. After he was given the vision, he blabbed to those around him. Then he had to go through what I will call the "pit season". After he prematurely ran with this new and profound dream, he had to go through a process. A humbling and painful process of being in the pit of despair numerous times, and then being rescued by God. So why did God give it to him so early? There are times when God gives you a dream that only the person you'll grow to be can fulfill it. It is the time between now and then that will make you exactly who you need to be.

Unfortunately, that novel I wrote years ago was never published. In fact, it was rejected. At the time it felt terrible, but it got me comfortable with knowing that rejection is part of life. We can't be afraid to fail. The problem was, I got the vision and I forgot to steward it. I told people prematurely, didn't take the time to pray, work, and let God cultivate the vision first. I had become so excited that I mistook the vision for the end goal. I thought the book was the end goal, but he had an ever greater goal of changing me, and making me stronger. What did I learn from the process? I learned that I hadn't even asked God if I was supposed to write a romance novel or a Bible study. I just assumed He would have me writing romance, since I love the idea of love.

Like most amazing and wonderful things in life, there is a process that makes the work wonderful and amazing. Books have stages of outlines, rough drafts, editing, and re-editing. Think of the world's best chocolate cake. It didn't start out the best. It doesn't even start as cake. It starts as different things that have to be mixed, broke, opened, cracked, stirred. Even after all that, it could still turn out as a burnt chocolate cake. Who can really say for sure when the process is done, except the one who gave you the vision, your Maker. My point is that no matter where you are in the process, remember that God will fulfill his purposes for you.

1. Read 2 Samuel 7. Describe David's vision and dream. Write down what was good about it. Then write down why God didn't allow him to accomplish his dream in the way David thought things should work. What do you learn from this?

2. Have you had a dream or desire that hasn't worked out yet? Write this down. How is God either pointing you towards something else, or preparing you for the right time?

3. Think of a time where you failed at something. What went wrong? What did you learn from this experience, and how has it allowed you to become stronger?

Fishing

Do you like to fish? Thousands of dollars are spent each year on trying to catch fish. There's a more important kind of fishing that we have been called to. It's the fishing of souls. In Jeremiah 16, the Lord tells his people that he will send fishers of men, or those who will go to reach the souls of others. Jesus called his disciples to follow him, and said he would make them fishers of men. They thought they were doing well as fishers of fish, but he had an even greater role for them. Now, If we are called as fishers of men (and every follower of Jesus is), then how do we do it well?

First, focus on God instead of your circumstances. It's easy to lose sight of what God has called us to do when we focus on our circumstances. Do you remember what happened to Peter? He believed that Jesus could enable him to walk on water. As he was walking towards Jesus on the water, he took his eyes off the Lord. He saw the waves, the wind, and the storm, and began to sink (Matt. 14:30). He needed this reminder that unless he was completely focused on the Lord, he would not be a good fisher of men.

Second, stir up the gift. If God calls us to cook for people, then start cooking. If God calls you to encourage people, then start speaking positively into people's lives. Whatever your gift is, stir it up. This means to start using it in any capacity. God will be beside you and will cultivate that gift you have the more you use it. In 2 Tim 1:6, Paul admonishes Timothy to fan (or stir up) the gift of God he was given. Evidently, Timothy had been reluctant to use and practice his gift. The church and others were missing out on the blessing of Timothy using it, as well as Timothy himself. If you are a Christian, know that God has given you a spiritual gift. He is calling you to use it, and not put it on the shelf. Just imagine a champion quarterback who sat on the sidelines, refusing to use his skills because he didn't feel like it. His team and the fans would suffer. Initially, you might not feel like using your gift, but if you work at stirring it up, it will be easier to practice.

The third point is that you must guard your heart. Anytime a gift is stirred up, it creates an opportunity for two problems: pride, and fear. There's no room for either. Pride happens when we forget that our gift comes from God. We must always remember that we tend to be glory thieves, stealing the glory that belongs to God alone. Fear comes when you put the opinions and thoughts of others above God's. When you care more about what others think of you than what God thinks, you will find yourself in trouble.

Fourth, serve God and help all you can. The disciples weren't qualified in a way that the world would consider qualified. Paul himself pointed to his weaknesses as proof of his qualifications, not his strengths. You may not be a success in how the world describes it, but that's ok. The world doesn't define your ultimate success. God does. In his eyes, success is serving him and helping others. So go fishing today. Don't worry about how quickly you see success. You may never see it. If you are faithful, then God will ensure your ultimate success.

1. Read 2 Corinthians 3:4-6. In what ways are you tempted to claim sufficiency by your own merits or resume? What does Paul teach us about true sufficiency?

2. Read 2 Cor. 4:7-18. On a piece of paper, make 2 columns. For one, write "my weaknesses" and for the other,

"God's answers." Then go through the passage and write what you see for each in the appropriate columns. What did you learn?

3. Read 2 Cor. 12. What does the chapter say about Paul's strengths and weaknesses? Why did God give him a thorn in the flesh? What are 3 things you learn from this chapter?

Saying Yes to Compassion

You know my friends, there are many shades to every person. I think we all have the potential to be either really awesome, really awful, or somewhere in between. Most of us fall on the scale of awesome in some places and then maybe awful in a few others. I call that normal. Myself? Well let's just say if there were to be a shortage of diet coke and coffee the same day that I have a migraine, then watch out. Pretend that this shortage and the migraine comes the very day after I have been up all night cramming for a test, or up all night with my kids during a stomach virus epidemic. The result would be quite possibly, the very worst version of me. I am not going to be the usual, outgoing, joyful lady I tend to be. No, just the opposite. But I know this. The fact that I know my weaknesses gives me an advantage.

Do you know your weaknesses? Let's talk about another scenario: what if it is that time in the month where as a woman it is a rough time...girl you know what I am saying? Then there just happens to be a pan of brownies on the stove. It is a recipe for trouble for some of us. I will be like, " Please someone get that pan away from me." But again, I know this about me, and that gives me the advantage. Advantage over who? The enemy, our adversary, the devil. You better believe he knows your weaknesses just like mine. He has weaknesses too, like exposure, praise, and truth. I like exposing the schemes of the enemy for what they really are, trickery. Tricks to get us to hurt ourselves or others.

But given the right circumstances and depending on the area of life that we are being tested in, it can make for a prime opportunity for the flesh to take over. When the flesh takes over, two things can happen. First, we act in a way that is sinful even when we know it is wrong. Afterward, any number of things start trying to take root without us noticing. A type of evil sneaks in a little at a time. Secondly, our thinking goes wrong so that we can spiral downhill. When we allow our flesh to have opportunity, we place ourselves in spiritual danger. It's like heading into a battle unarmed. Who would do that? Yet, we do it when we are not spiritually prepared for war. Our enemy is not our neighbor, spouse, friend, child, etc. You have one enemy, Satan. It may feel like you have other enemies, but your number one enemy is the evil one.

What should you do when you recognize good aspects and not so good aspects in your character? How do we overcome the temptation to give into the flesh? How do we stop it? Most of all, how can you and I be encouraged to keep changing, and not grow discouraged? First and foremost, in any moment of weakness, know that you are human. I am not condoning sin, nor am I giving you the go ahead to be hateful or eat that pan of brownies. What I am saying is that as humans, we come face to face with our weaknesses and imperfections. This wasn't the way God designed us, but is a result of the fall. In our human nature, we have the propensity to give into the flesh. The good news, the news that I want you to remember, is that Jesus the God-man lived the perfect human life in our place. He died and credited his righteousness to our account, so that we could be released from the slavery of sin.

Second, remember that God loves you. I know he loves me. Remember no one is perfect, or without sin. When you do sin, quickly take it to God. Better yet go to God in that center stage where sin makes its grand entrance. He will give you a way out. How can we fight our flesh, pride, and fear with compassion?

Well, it has been my experience that during a fight with my sinful flesh, the enemy will strategically place a person who struggles with pride in my presence. Why? Perhaps this is because my sin increases their pride and their judgement fuels my response. The good news is, this attack can be stopped! Compassion can cancel any assignment from the enemy quicker than you can say, "praise the Lord". Now we can't force a prideful person to have compassion, but we can have compassion on others and pray for their pride to be broken.

1. In what areas of your life are you strong in showing compassion? In what areas do you need to grow? Write down 3-5 specific areas for each one.

2. Compassion is not a personality problem. Compassion is actually a worship problem. Read Ephesians 1:3-5, and Luke 7:47. How does God's love for us motivate and enable us to show compassion to others?

3. What are some truths from 1 Pet. 1:22-25 that teach us about the nature of biblical love and compassion?

4. What is the link between pride and the lack of compassion?

5. Write down 3 ways in which you could show compassion to someone today.

Reconciliation

Jesus never fails. He is always there for us when we need him. If only other people were the same. It seems that our parents and family members can hurt us, without even knowing it, and yet God calls us to still forgive them. I've heard many sermons on forgiveness and reconciliation, arguing that you don't have to do both. My question though is, "if you still feel the tinge of disgust at the thought of reconciliation, then have you really forgiven them?" Jesus comes to rescue us and heal our hurt. If you hold onto unforgiveness because it's become the normal for you over the years, then all you are doing is wrapping that little wound with a band aid of bitterness. Consider this story of forgiveness and how it could change the way you view forgiveness and reconciliation.

In Matthew 18, after Jesus tells his disciples what it looks like to address sin in the life of another believer, Peter asks 1 of his "what about" questions. What about if my brother keeps sinning against me, and keeps asking forgiveness, how long do I have to keep forgiving him? While the Jewish Rabbis believed God only forgave 3 times, and therefore they only had to, Peter thought 7 times would be more than plenty (18:21). He thought he would impress Jesus by his generosity in forgiving. But Jesus blows him out of the water by his answer. Jesus's response focuses on God's unlimited forgiveness of us, that doesn't stop when we hit a certain limit. We are called to forgive in this same way.

Jesus then tells the disciples a story, or a parable to drive home the point. The main point of the parable is not how much the debt is in today's dollars, or how the servant ended up with this debt. His point is in verse 35: Forgiven people forgive others. A refusal to forgive others can indicate that you haven't aren't forgiven. The story starts off with a king, who represents the Father. This king is owed a great debt by his servant. The time comes to settle accounts and the books are opened. His servant owes a massive debt toward the king, one that is unpayable. The disciples instantly understood the debt was unpayable. 10,000 was the largest number in greek. It would be like saying in our time a zillion dollars or a goggleplex dollars-the largest number you could think of.

The king had the right to throw the servant in debtor's prison for failing to pay. Remember at this time there were no bankruptcy options, no debt consolidation plans. If you couldn't pay, you could be thrown in debtor's prison and your family members sold to pay off the debt. Debtor's prison's were not a good way to deal with debtors who were willing to pay-repayment in them was almost impossible. They were only used as last resort. What's crazy is that the servant thinks he can pay it back. He pleads for the king to give him more time. But we all know he's lying. He couldn't live enough lifetimes to pay it back. Amazingly, the king forgives him and releases him from the debt. No repayment plan is required. As the servant goes out and tells others, he runs into a fellow servant who owes him a good deal of money. On a horizontal level, the person to person level, he is owed a good deal of money. If someone borrowed $5 from you, you wouldn't worry about it. But if they borrowed $5000, you better believe you would care about getting it back. So on the horizontal level, it was a lot, but compared to what he was forgiven, it was a penny in a portapotty.

The other servant pleads with him for patience, but it's like he doesn't even think about how he was forgiven. He throws the other servant in debtor's prison until he will repay. When the other servants hear about it, they are greatly disturbed. They go back to the king and report what happened. The king calls back in the servant, and lets him know the debt is back on. What do we learn from this story? We learn that forgiven people forgive. A failure to forgive brings into question whether or not we are forgiven.

1. Is there anyone in your life you need to forgive? Write their name down.

2. Forgiveness is not a feeling, rather it's a promise. It's a promise:

    •   I will not bring this sin up to myself.
    •   I will not bring this up to you to hurt you with it.
    •   I promise not to bring it up to others.

    What part of this promise do you struggle with?

3. Read Matt. 18: 21-35. What do you learn about the king and the servant from this parable?

God's Presence

To set the scene, you should know that this particular story in the Bible takes place during Solomon's reign. Solomon was David's son. Do you remember King David? David was one of the best kings of Israel. He started off as a simple shepherd, but God brought him all the way to king. David is described as a man after God's own heart. He loved God and served him, while at times doing some pretty bad things. He had a son named Solomon. David wanted Solomon to walk with God and enjoy God's presence as he did. The key was that Solomon needed to obey God in all things.

Our story begins when Solomon becomes king. God appears to him in a dream, and asks him the question that we would all love to be asked. God asks Solomon what he would like. Oddly enough he didn't want riches, wealth, or honor. He didn't even want revenge on his enemies! Solomon asks for wisdom. His request pleased God so much that he also gave Solomon riches and honor. You can read about this story in 2 Chronicles 1:7-13.

The chapter starts off with describing how God was with Solomon in his kingdom, and made him exceedingly great (1:1). Notice that it was God who made Solomon great. Solomon had to work and fulfill his role, but it was God who magnified him, and grew his kingdom. God's promises to Solomon were both conditional and unconditional. No matter what Solomon did, God was going to give him wisdom. At the same time, long life was promised to Solomon, but only if Solomon walked in the ways of God. Solomon started off well. He enjoyed God's presence and the blessings that came from obeying God. He soon ran into trouble, however.

Solomon disobeyed God in several areas. He multiplied wives and horses, which was what God said not to do. His many wives pulled him away from the worship of the true God into idolatry. Eventually, Solomon's kingdom was hurt by his actions. After Solomon died, God split up his kingdom. We read of Solomon's life experiences in the book of Ecclesiastes. Solomon describes how he could not find happiness in anything in life, apart from God. If he could send you a message today, Solomon would say, "Obey and follow God, and enjoy the blessings that come from a closeness to the Lord."

God's presence is one of the best gifts he gives us. One of the best promises in Scripture is Hebrews 13:5-6. Here, God promises to never leave or forsake us. He promises us his presence. Other people will leave and forsake you. Other people won't give you the gift of their presence. God is not like that, however. His presence and nearness is the best gift you can recieve.

1. Read Hebrews 13:5-6. In what ways does this verse encourage you?

2. What other stories or verses in the Bible remind you of God's presence? Write some of these down here.

3. How have other people let you down? What biblical passages remind you of God's character, and that he never will leave you or fail you?

4. If you are struggling with believing God is present, write your prayer down here with a request for help.

Annette D. Burke

Keeping Joy

A dear friend told me that the one thing she wanted the most was to learn how to have joy in all circumstances. No matter what was going on around her, she wanted to be joyful. As I pondered on this, I was left wondering how we find that joy? I know that we find our joy in Christ, but how do we keep that joy? How do we remain joyful when our spouse says something hurtful? How do we remain joyful when we are in emotional, spiritual, or physical pain? One answer is having the right perspective.

In James 1:2, we read, "Consider it pure joy, my brothers and sisters, whenever you face trials of many kinds." Why does James say this? He adds, "for you know that the testing of your faith produces steadfastness. And let steadfastness have its full effect, that you may be perfect and complete, lacking in nothing." James knows that the testing of our faith has an effect on our joy. It can deepen and strengthen it, so that when stronger storms and trials come, we are able to withstand them. We see this in life. Do you know any of those positive people, who just seem to have a great outlook on life? Well, guess what they are doing...they are counting it all joy!

Imagine that you're washing dishes and crying (because of any number of reasons we women cry), when all of a sudden this beautiful, iridescent bubble floats right up in front of your face. Its transparency reminds you of your vulnerability, and for some crazy reason you are fascinated. There are so many beautiful colors! Now, you took a moment to relish in the simple beauty of the silly little iridescent bubble, and have forgotten how bad things were in the first place. On top of that, you are no longer crying!

I would encourage you to find beauty in the simple things. Stop getting so overwhelmed with things you can't control, like other people for example. Though you are beautiful when you cry, a smile on your face is so much better!

1. What things or areas do you find yourself feeling overwhelmed in? What are 2-3 ways in which you could focus on something else that reminds you of God's care and concern for your life?

2. Phippians is a book about joy. Paul speaks of joy a number of times. What situation and circumstance is he writing from? How is this surprising to you?

3. The next time you are tempted to complain, ask yourself, "Where can I find joy in this situation?" What is your answer?

The Feels

I am a feeler. I mean that through and through. For most of my life, how I feel has dictated what I think and how I act. I am not proud of that, but it is true. Now having to "adult" most days means there is tons of stuff that has to be done, no matter how I feel. An example of this is if you have an argument with someone. Let's say I got into some heated words with a very good friend. Following the argument, all I want to do is cry and lash out with hatefulness at everyone around me. But deep down, I know that even if I feel that way, sowing seeds of hatefulness will only produce more heated words in the future with my loved ones. I don't want that, especially when they didn't cause the hurt to begin with! So my question for you today is, "what do we do when our feelings don't line up with what we know?"

Many people would look to their heart. Follow your heart, they say, and you'll be happy. Do whatever your heart feels like, and you'll be fine. The problem with this is, our heart. In Jeremiah 17:9, we read that, "the heart is deceitful above all things, and beyond cure. Who can understand it?" So first of all, I know that my heart can lie to me. If it is deceitful, then listening to my feelings all the time is like listening to a liar. While our feelings make good cabooses, they don't make good engines. We don't want to ignore our feelings, but we have to be careful not to be led by them.

What should you do when you don't feel like doing something you should, or feel like doing something you shouldn't? First, remember that God changes our feelings and emotions. Sanctification is the process of becoming more like Christ. In this process, God changes our hearts and our emotions. We want to be honest with our feelings and bring them before God. Then, we want to ask him to change our feelings so that they are pleasing to him. We may need to do what is right (or not do what is wrong) even when our feelings tell us the opposite.

Developing godly feelings is like building a fire. It takes time and effort. You don't get there right away. By thinking about the right things (Phil. 4:8), and feeding our minds with God's truth, we help to build godly emotions. By the same token, when we avoid listening or taking in things that are negative, false, or hurtful, we also help strengthen godly feelings.

1. Do you tend to follow your feelings? Describe the results, both positive and negative.

2. What feelings can you see in your life that need adjusted or changed? What are some truths of God's Word that you can use to correct those feelings?

3. Feelings and emotions are good. How can you use your right feelings and emotions to serve God and others this week?

Annette D. Burke

Faith

Faith is knowing and believing that God's word is true, and his love is real. Simply put, faith is pressing forward, it is clinging and holding confidently to God's promises regardless of how I feel. In Hebrews 11:1, we have one of the best definitions of faith. This verse says, "Now faith is the assurance of things hoped for, a conviction of things not seen." Faith is your shield. Faith is what keeps your chin up when Chicken Little says, " The sky is falling!" Faith is what keeps joy in your heart even when an illness is merciless on your body.

Faith is what enables you to love your children even when they scream that they hate you, or don't call you for weeks. Faith is what gives you the get up and go when your car is broken down, and you only have a five dollar bill to your name. Yes friends, I've been there. Years ago, during a horrendous custody battle, I thought financially I would never make it. I wasn't sure if I would keep my babies and have a place to live. I didn't have any furniture, but I had God. I had faith. Now that seems like a dream. I listen to my family downstairs, as I sit in my cozy office, and find it hard to believe that I ever slept on the floor. I prayed one thing back then, that God would overwhelm me with his power, and not my circumstances. He did. I think that the biggest hindrance to faith is fear and unbelief. I still get afraid, but I have learned that I have control. I can act out my faith and my thoughts will follow.

In Proverbs 30:5, we read that God says He is a shield to those who take refuge in Him. You might be going through something currently that is testing your faith, or you will be. Regardless, God has a plan to grow your faith. Like a tree, you won't grow larger or stronger if you are not tested. The promise of God is that he strengthens our faith. He provides us with the grace we need to remain true and faithful to him.

This week, I'd like you to think more deeply about your faith. When fear, doubt, and unbelief set in, run as fast as you can back to the promises of God. You'll grow your faith as you meditate on God and his Word.

1. What promises of God in Scripture bring you hope and strength? Write them here.

2. Read Hebrews 11. This chapter is called the faith chapter. Write down all the ways you see in which people displayed faith despite their challenges.

3. Pick 1 attribute or characteristic of God this week to think about. Look up as many verses as you can about this attribute or characteristic. How does this help strengthen your faith?

Blessed

It seems that we all want to be blessed. And our God does graciously bless us, even if it is sometimes hard to see. If you are going through your days and it seems there are no blessings for you, and you're wondering why God doesn't seem to be throwing anything good your way, what can you do? The best answer is look to the Word of God, and read about His blessings. We see the blessings of God described all over Scripture. I've searched my Bible and found lots of blessings that God promises us today in return for actions that glorify Him. Here are a few examples.

1. Don't listen to the Word as simply a nice suggestion, rather do what it says... then God will bless you for doing it. James 1:22a and 1:25b.
2. Give generously... not grudgingly for the Lord your God will bless you. Deuteronomy 15:10.
3. Be obedient and you will be blessed. Deuteronomy 28:2.
4. Be godly and you will be blessed. Psalm 5:12.
5. Fear the Lord. Psalm 115:13
6. Have your strength in the Lord. Psalm 84:5.
7. Patiently endure testing and temptation and you will be blessed. James 1:12.
8. Bring in all your tithes and He will pour out a blessing so great. Malachi 3:10.
9. Realize your need for Him. Matthew 5:3.

These are just some of the ways I found that we can strive to do our part, in order to receive a blessing. Give God the glory, and in return, He promises His blessings upon us. Keep your motives focused on God and doing these things for Him, and He will give you what His Word promises. I don't mean that God gives us everything we want. We reject the teaching that says if you name it and claim it, God will give it to you. Or, the teaching that says anything we lack is because of a lack of faith on our part. God hasn't said these things. He isn't required to bless us in any way, but he does. This is what we call grace.

Today, there is a simple place to start. Begin with prayer and reading the Word. Then take what you hear to heart, to do what it says. God blesses our obedience to him. You might not see it today, or this week, but blessings will come. So keep doing, trusting, and obeying him, and you will receive his blessings.

1. Read Psalm 1. What blessings do you see come from following God? How would your life be different if you looked like the tree planted by the rivers of water?

2. Read Galatians 6:6-10. What warnings and encouragement do you see from this passage? When do we see fruit from our work? Why are we told not to grow weary. Write down 3 ways in which you can obey this passage.

3. What area of your life would you like to see God bless? Craft a prayer asking him for help in this area, while thanking him even if he doesn't answer your prayer as you would like.

Insulted

Now I would love to sit here and write to you that to every person who insults me, I'm able bless their socks off. But...I can't. For me, insults are like trying to eat ice-cream in the heat. Sometimes stuff gets messy. Worst of all, it just leaves me sticky. I think the first insult I ever had was when I was like 6. The scene is kindergarten. We are sitting playing, and this girl says, "You have a big nose. I don't like you." My reply was, "Well, you stink." I remember thinking, "Ha! Take that mean girl!" You can guess the rest; she said another mean thing then so did I. It just kept going. Unfortunately, that has not been my only childish spat. I am very much an adult now, but I still feel this deep protective instinct to lash out in return when someone deeply insults me.

So I pray, I fast, I ponder over this "being insulted" thing. Through the years, God has done a great work for me when it comes to offenses. I am for the most part, not easily offended. There is however one exception to the rule, which is my immediate family or those I am closest to. Have you ever had your spouse or one of your parents say something to you and it just shakes you? Or your kids speak nonsense to you and it just hurts in such a way that you feel the right to defend yourself?

I like to analyze. I analyze my behavior and try to figure out why I react in a certain way. I realized that my reactions stem from my desires. They stem from this deep desire to receive love from others. While that is a good desire, it can go wrong if I sin in order to get it, or sin when I don't get it.

As I was reading in God's Word, I came across 1 Peter 3:9.

He says, "Do not repay evil with evil or insult with insult. On the contrary, repay evil with blessing, because to this you were called so that you may inherit a blessing." I tried to wrap my brain around this verse for a week. I told God in my prayers, "How can we truly do this? Lord, are you saying just to let everyone walk all over us? Well, I just can't do it. Period. End. Done. Anything else I will do, but I just can't bless someone who I feel isn't respectful of me." Then it happened. I was insulted. Not a little, but a lot. You know those tender spots you get? Like if you were chunky as a kid, and someone mentions weight, you get fired up? I didn't bless the person who insulted me. I also didn't bless the next person who came along. My attitude was insulting to them. Do you see how the cycle goes?

Later that day, still feeling down, I heard a song, now revised, but originally written by the hymn writer Fanny Crosby. It went, "O what a Savior, wonderful Jesus." I thought, "That's it! I realized that we don't win by insulting back, but by blessing back. How can we do this? Only by having the grace of Jesus in our lives. He is the firm foundation that allows us to bless those that hurt us.

Next time, I want to direct my anger where it belongs. I want to praise God for every insult that gives me an opportunity to hate the devil and love God more. I am praying for you today. I am praying that you would stand firm too. I pray that your heart be guarded by grace with the next insult or feeling of rejection that comes your way.

1. Read Romans 12:9-21. Love bookends the beginning and ending of this passage. Write down what you learn about love and how we are called to treat those who mistreat us. What are some applications for your life?

2. Rewrite Rom. 12:9-21 as a prayer. In it, make it personal and applied to your life situation.

Hidden Treasure

Now typically, genealogies seem a bit boring. Especially if it isn't your own bloodline. There are nine chapters taking up residence in 1 Chronicles when, boom, all of a sudden hidden treasure breaks out. Hidden treasure? Yes. It is a small part, but a powerful blessing. Here we read in 1 Chronicles 4:9-10, "Now Jabez was more honorable than his brothers. His mother called his name Jabez saying, "Because I bore him in pain." And Jabez called on the God of Israel saying, "Oh, that You would bless me indeed, and enlarge my territory, that Your hand would be with me, and that you would keep me from evil, that I may not cause pain. So God granted him what he requested."

Isn't it so intriguing that the writer of this passage chose to stop, change things up for a minute, and then go back to the previous listing of the genealogy? The prayer of Jabez isn't meant to be a magical prayer that God is obligated to answer. It isn't a sure fire way to get what we want. If we aren't careful, it can become a type of vain repetition that Jesus warns us about in the sermon on the mount.

At the same time, this passage is a hidden reminder of how God blesses those who obey him. The Bible has all kinds of hidden treasure in it, little places that speak to our current trials and situations.

1. This week, look for hidden treasure in your Bible reading. What is one treasure from each daily reading

that you can write down, and think about throughout the day?

2. Craft a simple prayer to God asking him for help in one area of your life. Keep it simple so that you can reflect on this prayer throughout the day.

Annette D. Burke

Check Yourself

In the honor of transparency, let it be known that I am not the master at modeling a good attitude. I have learned to allow God to work in me and through me by having disciplined myself to spend time with him. I have also learned to be kind in my mind. Specifically, what I mean by that is, don't beat yourself up. If you mess up or behave in a way that is unbecoming, confess your sin to God and others, repent, and embrace the Lord's forgiveness.

Don't sit around and loathe yourself. Don't allow yourself to say things like, "you are terrible, or, "you are a horrible person," because that is not kind. It is ok to say things like, "that was a terrible way to act," or, "that was a horrible way to behave." Do you see the difference? I know that the minute I start to drift towards other negative thoughts, my attitude will drift as well. Then before you know it, you are bitter. Follow me here. This is a whole mood. The day starts, you mess up, you rally in a bit of self loathing. Next thing you know, lethargy and depression have set in your heart. It's time for your family or friends to come around, and your entire mood of hatefulness spills over onto them. Have you heard the saying, "It's a slow fade"? That is so true! You didn't start out the day hoping to be a sour apple to everyone. It started with you thinking wrongly of God and yourself.

Psalm 14 reminds me of this, and how important it is to know that God and his love doesn't just change our lives, but also the lives around us too. For example, in Psalm 14:4 we read, "Have they no knowledge of all the evildoers who eat up my people as they eat bread, and do not call upon the Lord?" We know two things about the people David is describing. First, they are negatively affecting others (devouring). Second, they do not seek God.

Good sense tells me that the opposite would be true as well. If I seek God, I will positively affect others. Instead of devouring, I will be embracing them. In Galatians 5, we are warned about devouring others. Checking ourselves means that we think about how we are viewing and treating others, as well as ourselves. Are we living like a child of God, an image bearer of him? Or, are we living like an image bearer of the evil one? God would have us think rightly of ourselves. Not that we are worthless, and not that we are that great. Instead, that we belong to an awesome God. As we do, we will be able to treat others in the right manner.

1. Read Galatians 5. How can we use our freedom in Christ to love others?

2. What goes wrong when we walk in the flesh instead of the Spirit?

3. In what areas is God calling you to put off walking in the flesh? What do you replace these with?

Rose

Have you ever had one of those average-blah-yuck-can't-complain-day (BYCCD)? I have had plenty. It is the kind of day where you know there is beauty in your life, but you still feel like it's less than what you want. It's meh. I find that those days are the days where I can miss the really awesome things God is doing in my life. I am lacking zeal and prone to notice imperfections. Here's an illustration of BYCCD, but with a rose. A rose has roots, a stem, leaves, thorns, and hopefully a bud. For one thing, what does the stem do? There is a scientific way of explaining this, but for us I am going to granny style S'plain it to you. It puts space between the roses and thorns. It gives the needed space between the good and the bad in order for the nutrients to have the room they need to work their magic. What if your rose bud days and your thorn days were all lumped into one, and connected? Do you think that if our good-best-awesome days were all in rows we would appreciate them as much?

Oh, and the bad days. If I had all the bad days I have ever had, connected with no separation, I might not have survived. I have had some pretty bad days. The mundane days, the neutral ones, they give me time to just be. Today, I am reminded of how important those unimportant days are for our well being and our healing. I am going to celebrate those mundane days by thanking God for them. I want to ask you to thank God for your average-blah-yuck-but you can't complain days too. The BYCCD is where the magic is happening even if you can't see it. It's where the nutrients to your soul are sprouting rose buds.

1.   What benefits do ordinary days have?

2.   What would happen if every day was out of this world?

3.   Change happens in the ordinary moments, more than in the big ones. How is God changing you in your ordinary times?

4.   Craft a prayer of thankfulness such as:

God,

We know that the average and mundane day is necessary, just like the stem is necessary to a rose with thorns. We thank you for those days and the downtime, stability, and healing that they bring.

In Jesus name-Amen.

Rebuild

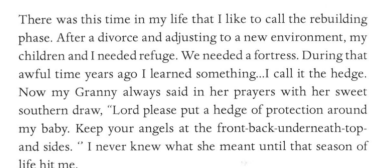

There was this time in my life that I like to call the rebuilding phase. After a divorce and adjusting to a new environment, my children and I needed refuge. We needed a fortress. During that awful time years ago I learned something...I call it the hedge. Now my Granny always said in her prayers with her sweet southern draw, "Lord please put a hedge of protection around my baby. Keep your angels at the front-back-underneath-top-and sides. " I never knew what she meant until that season of life hit me.

It was her way of praying psalm 91:2, "I will say of the Lord, He is my refuge and my fortress: my God; in Him will I trust." I want to encourage you today to remember that no matter how bad what your going through feels, you do have a fortress. You do have a refuge. We have a real enemy and he would love for you to believe that you are all alone. Darkness would love for you to believe that your situation is hopeless, unfixable, and destitute. I want to tell you that is so far from the truth. There is only one thing required of you. Keep on trying to trust that God is good. It wasn't overnight, but God did fix my story. He gave it a beautiful twist. He brought joy back into our lives. He put the pieces back together for my family. There are no limits to God.

1. How have you seen God at work in your life or a situation? How has he turned things around in the past?

2. Read Psalm 107. How do you see God's glorious reversals of what seems to be hopeless situations?

3. Find a Psalm that connects to your situation, and rewrite it as a personal prayer.

Change

Have you ever woken up and thought, "Today, I am going to be better. I am going to do more." Maybe you thought about being more intentional about showing your spouse love. Maybe you thought that you would be more positive today. Or perhaps eating healthier and exercising. Now fast forward. It is almost bedtime, and you have had the day from darkness. You feel defeated because for reasons unknown to you, that cupcake was irresistible. Your spouse did that one thing that always gets on your nerves and you just lost it. Oh, and those kids, what toy did they not leave out for you to pick up? They were fighting and you could feel your blood pressure rising. Before you knew it, calamity was all around. How did this happen when you fully intended on being all you could be today?

I will tell you my friend. It happened because we are sinners. Apart from Jesus Christ, we can do nothing. But wait, maybe you have Jesus. Then what is the problem? We must surrender to him in all areas of our life, put off what is sinful, and put on what is right. On our own, we can't do this. We need his help. The good news of the gospel is that Jesus does this. He saves us, and saves us to change us.

1. Read Titus chapters 2 and 3. How do you see God's saving grace in these chapters? How do you see his changing grace?

2.   Read Romans 6. How do you see God's changing grace in this chapter?

3.   What areas of your life does God need to change? What is your role?

Calling

"If He has called you to it, He will see you through it."

Sometimes situations arise, storms brew, and things fester in our lives to test our shield of faith. We often don't understand these storms and things that happen. Even more so, we do not understand what God requires of us. How do we move forward during a hard trial in life? "By the word of truth, by the power of God, by the armor of righteousness on the right hand and on the left. (2 Corinthians 6:7).

We faithfully preach the truth in that God's power is working in us. We use the weapons of righteousness in our hands for attack and defense. When we pray, we must leave the doubt out of the prayer. We come boldly to the throne of the eternal, omniscient, and omnipresent God. Jesus reminds us of his father's love in the gospels, where he speaks about prayer. His message is that, "God, I trust you at this moment that when I prayed for a fish, you did not give me a snake. God, I trust you at this moment that when I prayed for an egg, you did not give me a scorpion. (Luke 11:1-13).

1. What verses and passages show us that God is a good heavenly father?

2.   What areas do you tend to doubt God in?

3.   Craft a prayer asking for God's help and goodness towards your situation, and fight with biblical hope that he will help you in it.

Rain Clouds

Pain is like a rain cloud. We know it's there, but yet when it unleashes a torrential downpour, more than just those right below the cloud get wet. Our fight with the neighbor or the parent in PTO, the disgruntled employee and/or customer may just be the effects of pain. Wouldn't it be easier to overlook some things people said, if we knew their external factors going on? Look for signs of others' pain, maybe they are always slumped over, moody, distant; be the person who cuts them a break. Be kind to them, not because they deserve it, but because they are human beings just like us. More important than anything else is to have that kindness with your children. Let's pick our battles wisely. Life can change with one bad storm and we don't want to be left with only dreary days to remember. If we can't be kind to our own families, then are we really even nice at all?

So I dare you be the umbrella and not the rain. Maybe you're neither and you just always seem to be in a bad way. You're the lump with bad luck who is always in a storm. This verse is for you: The Lord will fight for you, and you have only to be silent. -Exodus 14:14. Remember, life occurs in seasons, so even though it feels like we're always the unlucky ones. Thank goodness the seasons are always changing! So no matter where we're at in life something is bound to change. God will help you in the storms of life. He cares about each person so much that he wants to build our character. It is up to us on how to rise to the occasion.

1. Where is the pain in your life? How can this pain point you back to your heavenly Father?

2. How does looking at the circumstances and situations of others allow us to have more patience with them?

3. What season of life are you in right now? Describe how God's grace is sufficient for it.

Annette D. Burke